Great Things to Make and Do for 6 Year Olds

KINGFISHER BOOKS
Grisewood & Dempsey Inc.
95 Madison Avenue
New York, New York, 10016

First American edition 1994
10 9 8 7 6 5 4 3 2 1
© Grisewood & Dempsey Ltd. 1994

Library of Congress Cataloging-in-Publication Data
Manley, Deborah.
    Peppermint mice : great things to make and do for six year olds
/ by Deborah Manley.
        p.   cm.
    1. Handicraft--Juvenile literature.   2. Games--Juvenile
literature. [1. Handicraft.   2. Games.]   I. Title.
TT160.M347   1994
745.592--dc20   93-23330   CIP   AC

ISBN 1-85697-928-8

Design and illustration by the Pinpoint Design Company
Printed in Great Britain

Peppermint Mice

Great Things to Make and Do for 6 Year Olds

Deborah Manley

Kingfisher Books

NEW YORK

CONTENTS

HANDY TIPS

Transform a walnut shell into a tiny tortoise, or make a beautiful necklace out of old aluminum foil. With a little imagination, a lot of household throwaways can be used to make all kinds of weird and wonderful things.

Start a collecting box...
Keep your eyes open
for possible materials
and store them in a box
or bag.

• Old Christmas or
birthday cards and cereal
boxes are a good source of
lightweight cardboard.

• Old magazines, postcards, and newspapers can be cut up and used for collages and pictures.

• Pieces of string and yarn are always useful.

• Add old straws, bits of elastic, yogurt containers, left-over scraps of material, and buttons to your collecting box.

Tools to work with
Here are some of the tools
that you will need:

- a pair of scissors
- a ruler
- a hole punch and a stapler
- tape
- pencils, crayons, and felt-tip pens
- an eraser and a pencil sharpener
- paints
- glue—white glue is best for making models, but
you can also use glue sticks for gluing paper
and thin cardboard. Whatever kind of glue you are
using, remember to give it time to dry.

Getting ready
Now that you have all the materials ready, you
need somewhere to work.

- Always make sure that you
have plenty of room—a clear
table top is ideal, but cover it
with newspaper first.

- It is a good idea to cover
yourself with an old shirt or
an apron.

Cleaning up
When you have finished, don't forget to clean up.

• Put all the lids back on your paints and on the glue bottle.

• Throw away any pieces of paper and cardboard that are too small to save.

• Put anything you haven't used back into your collecting box.

The ideas in this book are just a few of the things that you can make and do. Look for other useful materials such as bottle tops, old plastic bottles, old corks and matchboxes, and try out a few ideas of your own!

Family gallery

Draw or paint a picture of each member of your family and create your own picture gallery.

Dad   Mom

om   Mopsy

Bouncer

Swimmer

Polly

Me

Grandma   Granddad

HOPSCOTCH

You can draw a hopscotch game outside on the sidewalk or on a concrete playground.

You need:
a piece of chalk
a pebble for each
    player

You can play hopscotch on your own or with two or more players competing against each other.

To play, you throw your stone into the numbered squares in turn, starting with square 1. Then you hop along from square to square, leaving out the square with your stone in. On the way back, you bend down, pick up your stone, and hop out.

Here are some designs for you to use. With design A you put both feet down in squares 3 and 4 and squares 6 and 7, so long as your stone is not in them.

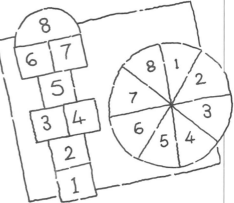

If you throw your pebble into the wrong square, or hop on a line, or can't pick up your stone, or fall over, then it is another player's turn. You start your next turn on the square that you ended your last turn in.

KEEP TO THE SQUARES

Some people think that when you walk along the sidewalk, you should only walk on the squares and not on the lines.

Why do they think this? Well, some people think that if you step on a line, you will turn into a frog. Other people think the bears will get you if you walk on the lines.

So, as you walk along, keep off the lines—make sure your foot always lands safely in a square!

When you're an expert at keeping off the lines, make it a little more difficult for yourself. Try hopping along, keeping off the lines. Try hopping first on one foot and then on the other.

Try taking a hop, then a step and then a jump, still keeping off the lines.

Be sure that you are walking in a safe place well away from the traffic. Cars and trucks are a *real* danger, not a make-believe one!

MAKE A MOBILE

When you make a mobile, you must take care to make each piece balance.

You need:
cardboard
drinking straws
a hole punch
thread
scissors

1. Draw some squares, triangles, and circles on cardboard. Make some big ones and some small ones. You can color them or draw designs on them if you want. Cut out the shapes.

2. Make a hole in each shape with the hole punch and tie threads of equal length through them.

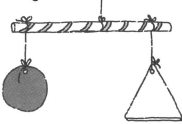

3. Tie one shape to each end of a straw. Tie another thread around the middle of the straw, and slide it along until you find that the shapes on either side hang level.

Now tie the loose end of this thread to one end of another straw. Then tie a shape to the other end of the straw so that the second straw balances.

4. Now tie a thread to the middle of this straw. When you hold it up, you should have a small mobile that balances. If one side is heavier than the other, push the threads along until it all hangs straight.

See if you can add more straws and shapes to your mobile.

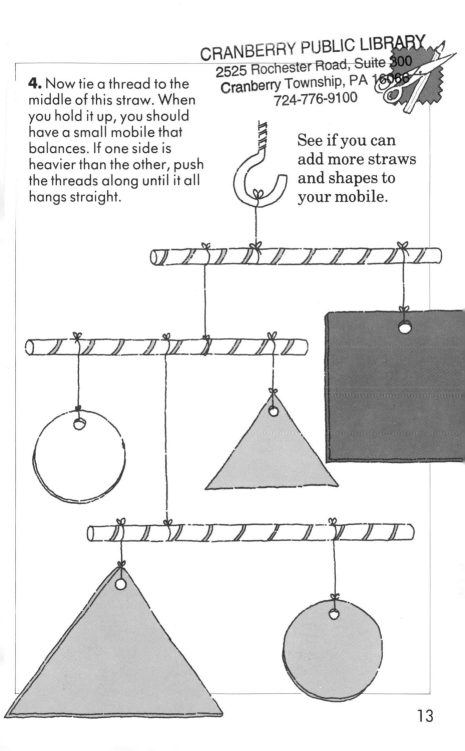

13

WHAT'S THAT NOISE?

Take turns with a friend to make sounds and guess what they are. Keep your eyes closed and listen carefully while your friend makes the sounds.

Here are some sounds you can make:

See how many sounds you can guess in a row. When you give up, let your friend become the guesser.

tear a sheet of newspaper
crumple up a piece of
    paper
rattle forks and spoons
    together
jingle coins together
tap the table with your
    fingers
tap the table with your nails
knock on a drawer
knock on the window
open a door
shut a door
shake keys
tap your toes on the floor
clap your hands
rub your hands against each
    other
knock on your head
yawn
turn on a faucet
pour water out of a
    bottle

QUIETLY, QUIETLY

If only two people play this game, one sits blindfolded on a chair while the other player creeps up silently from the far end of the room.

If the seated player hears anything, she points to the place the sound is coming from and says, "You're there!"

If she's right, the other player goes back to the start and begins again. If she's wrong, the other player continues.

If he reaches the blindfolded player without being heard, he wins. The players can then change places.

To play with a group, the players stand in a circle around the blindfolded player. One of them is chosen to creep up on the blindfolded player. If they are found out, someone else has a turn, but if they manage to reach the center, it is their turn to be blindfolded.

BE A JEWELRY MAKER

With some macaroni, some aluminum foil, and a paintbox you can make yourself some pretend jewelry to wear.

Macaroni jewelry

You need:
a bag of macaroni
paint and a brush
string

1. Paint the pieces of macaroni in different colors. Leave some in their own color.

2. Thread them onto string to make necklaces, bracelets, and anklets.

NOTE

If you have some wooden or other big beads, these could be strung in with the macaroni.

A silver chain

You need:
aluminum foil
scissors
a stapler

1. Cut strips of foil about 2 in. long by ½ to ¾ in wide. Make the first link by stapling the ends of a strip together.

2. Pass the next link through the first and staple it in the same way. Continue like this until your silver chain is long enough. (You can put a twist in some of the links so that they catch the light at different angles.)

Brooches

You need:
a circle of cardboard
    2 in. or more across
paint and a brush
a safety pin
tape

1. Paint the circle brilliant colors to look like gold and precious jewels. You can stick on some glitter if you have any.

2. When the paint is dry, put the brooch face down. Stick a safety pin to the back with tape.

NOTE

Brooches can be made in all sorts of different shapes and styles.

SHADOWS ON THE WALL

Shine a light against a wall. Now stand between the light and the wall to make shadow puppets with your hands.

Here's a turkey.

Here's a goose.

You only need one hand for a sheep.

This is a duck.

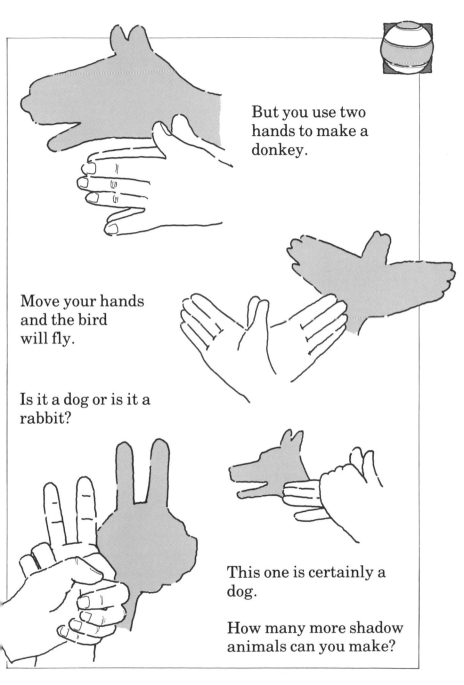

But you use two
hands to make a
donkey.

Move your hands
and the bird
will fly.

Is it a dog or is it a
rabbit?

This one is certainly a
dog.

How many more shadow
animals can you make?

GAMES FOR TRIPS

Here are some games to help pass the time on a long journey.

Sausages
One player is chosen to be IT and has to answer all the questions. But, whatever the others ask, IT must answer "sausages"—and he *must not laugh*, otherwise he is OUT!

What do you wear on your feet?

Sausages.

What's that on your head?

Sausages.

For example:

Who's your favorite rockstar?

Sausages.

Think up questions that make the answer as silly as possible to make the player laugh.

Ha ha ha ha ha ha
This is another game to make you laugh, but you must keep a straight face while you're playing it. Players take turns to pass on the laugh. The first player says "ha," the next "ha ha," and so on.

Name two

In this game players take turns to ask the others to give them the names of two of something. One player might say:

Name two animals.

The other replies:

Cat, dog.

You could ask for two people, two places, two flowers, and so on.

Color bingo

Prepare cards with colored squares as shown. Write the name of each color in the squares.

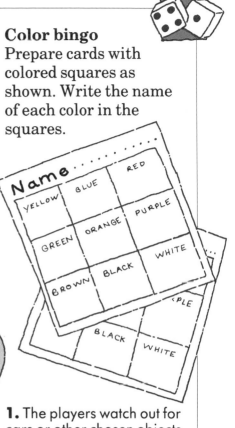

Name

YELLOW | BLUE | RED
GREEN | ORANGE | PURPLE
BROWN | BLACK | WHITE

BLACK | WHITE

1. The players watch out for cars or other chosen objects in those colors and put a cross in the right square when they see one.

2. A player who gets three crosses in a row wins a point.

3. The player who fills in a whole card scores three points. The player with the most points after several games is the winner.

HEADS, BODIES, AND LEGS

What could a cat-swan-man be? Find out when you play this game for two or more players.

You need:
paper
pencils

1. Each person has a sheet of paper and draws at the top of it the head and neck of an animal.

Try not to let the other players see what you are drawing.

2. Fold the paper over so that only the neck shows and pass it on to the next player.

NOTE

You can have fun making up names for the animals. You can also divide the feet from the legs to make an extra stage in the game.

---

3. Without looking at the heads, everyone draws the body and top of the legs of an animal onto the neck on the piece of paper they now have. Do not look at what has already been drawn on the paper.

4. Fold the paper again, so that only the top of the legs show, and pass it on to the next player.

5. Everyone now draws the legs and feet.

6. Pass on the papers once more and take turns opening up the pictures. See what strange and funny creatures have been invented!

Make a tortoise

Make a tiny tortoise to carry in your pocket.

You need:
a walnut
thin cardboard
a pencil
scissors
glue
paint or crayons

1. With an adult's help, open a walnut without breaking the shell. Lay half the shell edge down on the cardboard.

2. Draw around the shell, then add four legs, a head, and a tail.

3. Paint or color this shape to match the shell and carefully cut it out.

4. Glue this cutout firmly to the edge of the shell.

5. When the glue is dry, bend the tortoise's legs downward so that it can stand on the ground. Bend its head up a little so it can look around.

6. Now your tortoise is finished. Why not put a thread around its neck so that you can pretend it can walk?

A PICTURE MADE OF SEEDS

Collect seeds, such as rice and barley, dried peas or beans, lentils, orange and apple seeds, or melon seeds (dry these in the oven until they have brown stripes).

You can keep your seeds in an egg carton. Put a different kind of seed in each section.

You also need:
a piece of dark colored
   lightweight cardboard
a pencil
glue
a teaspoon

1. Draw a simple picture on the cardboard. One like this would work well.

2. Put glue on one small part of the picture. "Paint" that patch by pouring a few seeds from a teaspoon onto the glue. Glue another patch and paint it with other seeds.

3. When you have finished painting the whole picture with seeds, leave it to dry.

NOTE

If you want to preserve a seed picture, paint it over very thinly with clear varnish. Try not to let the varnish run off the seed onto the surrounding cardboard.

GROWING A BEAN

You need:
fresh lima or similar
   beans
a saucer
a flowerpot filled with
   soil
water

1. Start by putting your beans in a saucer of water and leave them for about three days.

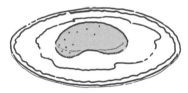

2. The beans will take in the water and begin to swell.

3. Now plant your beans in a flowerpot or a box of soil. Water the pot. Make sure the soil doesn't dry out while the beans are growing.

4. After about a week, dig up one bean. What has happened to it? Has it put down a root yet? Plant it again.

5. Dig up one of your beans every few days to see how the root is growing. Watch for the shoot to begin to grow upward.

Once the beans are growing through the soil, put a ruler in the flowerpot. Measure how quickly your beans grow each day.

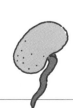

NOTE

The bean seedlings can be planted out in the garden when they are 3 to 4 inches high.

WHO IS THE FASTEST?

A running race is not the only kind of race you can try. Here are three others.

Hopping

Hop all the way on one foot. If you put the other foot on the ground, you have to go back to the beginning and start again.

Frog race

Squat down with your hands on the ground and hop like a frog.

Wheel race

Stand sideways to the way you will be going. With one step, swing your right foot across in front of you to face the opposite way. With the next stride, swing your left foot across behind you to face the way you began, and so on along the race track.

RACING BALLOONS

Play these two games for six players or more.

Down the row
Divide into two teams and sit in two rows facing each other with your legs stretched out in front of you as shown. Hold one hand behind your back.

Team throwing
Divide into two teams and form lines down the room. Each team has a balloon. The aim of the game is to be the first team to throw the balloon from one player to another down the line and back again. The balloon must be thrown and the players are not allowed to stand close enough to pass the balloon to each other.

Somebody tosses a balloon in between the rows. The players have to try and pat the balloon behind the backs of the other team. If they do, they score a point.

Make an animal mask

You need:
thin cardboard
a pencil
scissors
paint and a brush
elastic or string

3. Make two tiny holes at each side of the mask. Fasten thin elastic or string through the holes. The mask is now ready to wear.

1. Draw the outline of the mask on the cardboard. Add the fur and eye holes.

2. Cut out the mask and the eye holes. Now paint your mask in pussycat stripes.

NOTE

With a few changes you can make masks like this for a lion and a tiger, a dog and a wolf. Add long ears and—hey presto!—a rabbit.

Peppermint mice

Make a family of white mice with confectioners' sugar.

You need:
3 cups of confectioners' sugar
1 egg
juice from half a lemon
half a teaspoon of peppermint extract
a bowl and a sifter

1. Sift the confectioners' sugar into a bowl to remove all the lumps.

2. Ask an older person to separate the egg white from the yolk.

NOTE

If you have some food coloring, you could make different colored mice. You could also roll out the mixture and cut out circles and other shapes.

---

3. Mix the egg white and sugar together thoroughly and knead it with your fingers. Add the lemon juice a drop at a time until the mixture holds together.

4. Add the peppermint extract a drop at a time until you get the right taste.

5. Now knead the mixture with your fingers like putty. Mold it into sugar mice.

6. You could cut ears and tails from paper and stick them onto the mice. Mark the eyes with a toothpick.

7. Leave the mice overnight to harden—and hope that they don't run away before morning!

OB/TACLE COUR/E

Challenge your friends to an obstacle race! Here are a few ideas for obstacles. You can think up lots more of your own.

Balance a ball on a teaspoon and run with it.

Sit down and eat a dry cookie with a spoon and fork.

Crawl under a blanket laid out on the ground.

Put on some funny clothes and wear them to race to the finishing line.

Climb through the legs of a chair.

Struggle through a cardboard box.

Walk down a path blindfolded. Start again if you go off course.

GIANT STEPS

This is a game for at least four players.

Choose one player to be the caller. Everyone else stands in a line some distance away. The caller shows the players the different steps they may use in the game:

Giant steps:
the very longest steps that you can make.
Pin steps:
the very shortest steps that you can make on tiptoe.
Kangaroo steps:
leaping with feet together.
Hopping steps:
hopping along on one foot.
Frog steps:
squatting down and hopping along.

Then the caller calls out someone's name and tells them what kind of step they can take. For example, "Paul, take two giant steps." Paul must answer, "May I?" and then he can take two giant steps forward.

The caller gives everyone a chance to move forward, but if any of the players forget to say "May I?" they must go back to the start.

The player who reaches the leader first is the winner.

Chasing shadows

On sunny days, play with your own shadow and other people's.

Shadow tag
One player is IT and has to "tag" the others by stepping on their shadows.

Shadow changing
Make your shadow change shape as you bend and stretch and move around.

Leave your shadow
Usually your shadow starts right by your feet. But what happens if you jump very high? Can you escape from your shadow?

Short and long
When the sun is high in the sky, your shadow is short. As the sun sets, your shadow gets longer!

Watch a shadow
Your shadow is always changing because you run around. Choose something that stays still, like a plant, or a tree, or a toy. Watch its shadow shrink and grow through the day.

Ask if you can put a thermometer in a shady spot. Then put it into direct sunlight. How much hotter is one place than the other?

MAKE A BARK RUBBING

Each kind of tree has a different pattern on its bark. Make rubbings from the bark of trees and compare the different patterns.

You need:
paper
a dark crayon

1. Hold the paper over the bark of the tree. Rub the crayon gently over the paper. Soon you will see the bark pattern beginning to show through.

2. Take rubbings from other trees. Compare your bark rubbings. How are they different from one another?

NOTE

You can also make rubbings of coins, using paper and a crayon.

PICTURES FROM LEAVES

Make a collection of leaves. When you have collected a good selection, use them to make a leaf picture.

You need:
thickly mixed paint
white paper
newspaper
a paint brush
leaves

1. Look at a leaf. On one side it is smooth; on the other side you can feel the pattern made by the veins in the leaf. Paint this side of the leaf.

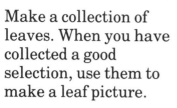

2. Then, very carefully, place the leaf, paint side down, on the white paper. Put some newspaper over it.

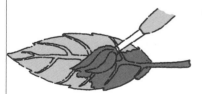

3. Press very gently with your fingers over the newspaper.

4. Lift the newspaper off carefully. Lift off your leaf and what do you find?

5. You can make all kinds of patterns with different leaves.

NOTE

Find out the names of the trees from which the leaves come and write them down beside a picture of each leaf. Learn to recognize the leaves from different trees.

FIND YOUR NAME

This is a good game to get a party started.

1. Write the names of your guests on a piece of construction paper in big letters.

2. Cut up each name into its separate letters.

3. Hide the letters around the room.

As your guests arrive, they have to look for the letters that make up their name. When they have found them, pin them onto the back of their clothes so everyone knows who's who.

NOTE

To make this game more difficult you can add last names so that everyone has two words to sort out. Try writing the first name in one color and the last name in another.

RED AND BLACK

This is a good card game for two players.

1. One player has the whole deck, face down. She holds up each card, one at a time, with its back to the other player. He has to guess if it's a red or a black card. If he's right, he keeps the card; if he's wrong, the first player keeps it for her own hand. In this way the two players divide the deck between them. Then the next part of the game begins.

2. The player who made the guesses puts a card face up on the table. The other player puts a second card face up beside it.

3. Then, in turn, the players put one card face up on top of the second card. They do this until a card with the same number as the first card is put on the second pile. Whoever put the card down can take all the cards on the table. Then they put down a new card to start a new round.

The person who collects all the cards is the winner.

FINGER THROWING

This is a guessing game for two players. You can play it anywhere—at home or when traveling.

1. Two players face each other, each with one hand made into a fist in front of them.

3. On "three," both players unclench their fists to show some or all of their fingers—or they can keep a tight fist so no fingers show. As they put out their hands, they guess how many fingers the other player will show.

2. One player counts:

ONE TWO THREE!

One! Two!

Three! Five!

NOTE

Use a pencil and paper to record the number of correct guesses.

4. The winner is the one who is first to guess correctly five times.

Make a telephone

Talk to a friend on your very own telephone.

You need:
two yogurt containers
a length of string (at least 10 to 13 feet long)

1. Make a hole in the bottom of each container. Tie a knot in one end of the string.

2. Thread the string through one container until the knot holds it. Then thread the other end through the other container and tie another knot.

3. Make sure the knots are big enough to stop the string pulling through the holes.

4. Each of you takes a container and moves far enough apart to pull the string tight.

5. Take turns to speak and listen.

Make a red meal

Plan a meal that will have as many red or reddish-brown colored things to eat as you can think of. You might choose a tomato salad, red jam tarts, and strawberry ice cream.

Here is a recipe for tomato salad.

You need:
one sliced tomato for each person
a teaspoon of brown sugar for each tomato
salt and pepper
a dish

1. Lay the tomato slices in a dish. Sprinkle the brown sugar, salt, and pepper over them. Leave the salad for at least an hour.

You could use a lettuce with red-tinged leaves for a salad, mixed with tomatoes and radishes. Or how about a pink colored meat, such as ham or salami.

Make a big pitcher of cranberry juice for a red drink.

Think about what you would serve if you gave a green meal, or a yellow one. You could even try a patriotic red, white, and blue one!

COLORFUL JAM TARTS

These jam tarts are made with different colored jams.

You need:

1½ cups all-purpose flour
7 tablespoons cold margarine
some ice-cold water
raspberry or strawberry jam (red)
apricot jam or marmalade (orange)
blackberry or blueberry jam (purple)
a bowl
a tablespoon
a cookie cutter
muffin pans

To make pastry shells:

1. Put the flour in a bowl. Cut up the margarine into little pieces. Blend them into the flour with the tips of your fingers until the mixture looks like breadcrumbs. You may need some help with this.

2. Add the water, a tablespoon at a time, until the mixture forms a ball.

3. Roll out the pastry on a floured surface. Cut out circles with a cutter. Put the circles into the bottom of the muffin pans, pushing the sides up all around. Put spoonfuls of the different jams into the pastry circles.

4. Bake your tarts in the oven for 10–15 minutes.

NOTE

The oven should be set at 375°F. The jam will be very hot when the tarts come out of the oven, so take care!

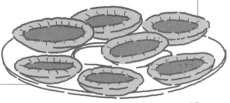

POT OF GOLD

Try this guessing game for two or more players.

One player thinks of an object. He says "If I found a pot of gold, I would buy . . ." and then describes a feature of the object.

The other players have to try and guess what the object is by asking more questions.

For example:
"If I found a pot of gold, I would buy something with two ears."
    "What color?"
    "Black and white?"
    "How many legs?"
    "Four."
    "A panda?"
    "No."
    "Bigger than a panda?"
    "Yes."
    "A horse?"
    "Yes."

THE LADYBUG GAME

In this game, each player tries to be the first to draw a ladybug.

You will need:
dice
pencils
paper

Each number on the dice corresponds to a bit of the ladybug's body.

Only when you throw the right number, can you draw that part of your ladybug. You will have to throw lots of fours to get all the legs.

1 = body
2 = head
3 = one spot
4 = one leg
5 = one eye
6 = one antenna

MAKE YOURSELF ON PAPER

You need:
a very large sheet of
    paper
a felt-tip pen
scissors
tape
a friend to help you

1. Tape pieces of paper together to make one really wide piece of paper (wallpaper lining is good).

2. Spread out the sheet of paper on a wide, flat, hard surface like the kitchen floor. You may need to put weights at the corners to stop it rolling up.

3. Lie down in the middle of the paper. Get comfortable so you won't need to move.

4. Now your friend can take the felt-tip pen and draw right round you in one single line. When the drawing is finished, get up and have a look at yourself.

5. Cut out your paper shape and pin it up in your room.

6. Draw around your hands to make outlines of them, too. Draw around your feet as well. Cut out these shapes and stick them onto the paper figure of your body.

Make a glove puppet

You need:
a piece of fabric (about
    8 inches x 5 inches)
a felt-tip pen
a needle and
    thread
two buttons for
    eyes
yarn for hair

1. Cut out two pieces of fabric like this, at the right size for your hand. Sew them together where the stitch marks are shown.

3. If your puppet is an animal, it will need ears. Cut these out from scraps of fabric. Sew them in as shown above when you sew the two pieces of fabric together.

2. Turn the glove shape inside out. Sew on the button eyes.
Add a nose and mouth with a felt-tip pen or stitch with yarn. Sew some loops of yarn hair around the head.

4. Put your hand inside your puppet. Your three middle fingers go in the wide body part and your thumb and little finger go into the puppet's hands. Talk to your puppet—before you know where you are it will be talking back to you!

More games for trips

Animal bingo

You need:
bingo cards
a pencil

Prepare a card for each player before you travel. The cards can have the names or pictures of animals on them.

1. The players watch for the animals on their card. When they see one, they point it out and tick if off on their card.

2. Each player who gets a row of three animals across, down, or from corner to corner scores a point. The first player to complete their card scores three points. The person with the most points after several games wins.

Silly shopping

Take turns to add something silly to the shopping cart.

1. The first player could say, "I went shopping and I bought a tiger and a bunch of bananas."

2. The second player might continue, "I went shopping and I bought a tiger, a bunch of bananas, and a car."

3. The game continues as long as you like. You can have a rule that a player who misses anything from the shopping list drops out. Or try buying things that all start with the same letter.

MAKE YOUR OWN JIGSAW

All you need to make your own jigsaw puzzle are two colorful postcards or cards, scissors, and an envelope.

1. Cut the cards into 10 or 12 pieces. You can use straight lines or wiggly lines, as you wish. Don't make any of the pieces too small.

2. Mix the pieces of card together in the envelope.

3. Now see how quickly you can sort out the two pictures and put them together again.

Ducks fly

This is a very funny game for four or more players. One person is chosen as leader.

The leader stands in front of the others and says, "Ducks fly," while she flaps her arms.

Quickly the others all flap their arms too.

The leader calls out more activities at a fast pace:

"Pigs grunt"—and she and everyone grunts.

"Horses gallop"—and everyone gallops.

But every now and then the leader tries to catch the others out by saying something wrong, such as, "Mice growl," and growling. Any player who growls is OUT.

ANIMAL GAMES

These are good party games because you need at least five friends to play.

One player is blindfolded and stands in the middle of the room.

Another player taps her on the back. "Who is it," asks the blindfolded player. "Ollie the Octopus," is the reply. The blindfolded player has to guess who Ollie is. If she's wrong, someone else taps her on the shoulder and she has to guess again. If she's right, Ollie becomes the guesser.

Quack! Moo!
Hide some small prizes, such as candies, around the room. The players divide into teams—ducks and cows—and choose two leaders.

The team members search for the hidden objects. When someone finds one, he or she has to make the correct animal noise to call their team leader over to collect it. The team that collects the most prizes wins.

Pig

You need:
a deck of playing cards
pencils and paper

The object is to be the first person to draw a pig. Each player is dealt five cards, face up. If he gets an Ace, King, Queen, or Jack, he can draw part of his pig for each of those cards, in this order: body, head, four legs (one at a time), and a curly tail.

If all the cards in the deck have been dealt and no one's pig is complete, shuffle the deck and keep on playing.

Fish tails

You need:
some newspaper
string

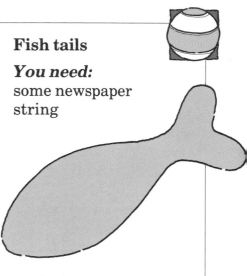

Each player tears out a fish shape about 8 inches long from newspaper.

Tie one end of a piece of string onto the fish and the other around each player's waist. The fish should lie flat on the ground. The players face each other and at "Go!" they try to "tag" each other by stepping on another player's fish.

51

Make fresh fruit kebabs

Make these delicious fruit salads on sticks with a variety of fruit pieces. You may need help preparing the fruit.

You need:
long toothpicks or
    wood skewers
a banana, sliced
some grapes
segments of an orange
some berries
    (strawberries, etc.)

NOTE

You can also use chunks of pineapple, and pieces of peaches or apricots.

You can make vegetable kebabs with tiny tomatoes, radishes, slices of cucumber, carrot and zucchini, and short pieces of scallions.

---

1. String the pieces of fruit onto the sticks. Put different kinds of fruit next to each other so that you get a good mixture of shapes and colors.

2. Serve your fruit kebabs with yogurt or ice cream.

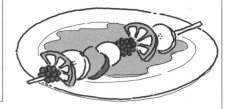

Grow a saucer garden

Here's a way to grow plants without planting any seeds at all. You grow the plants from the tops cut off root vegetables such as carrots, beet, and turnips.

You need:
the tops of carrots, turnips, and beet
a deep saucer or dish
some pebbles or gravel
water

1. Scatter the pebbles or gravel in the bottom of the dish. Lay the vegetable tops out on top. Pour water into the dish.

2. Make sure that there is always water in the dish. Now watch your saucer garden of vegetable leaves grow.

FIND THE PAIRS

This card game for two to four players will test your powers of memory!

The aim of the game is to collect pairs of cards with the same number or picture. For example, two tens, two Kings, and so on.

1. Spread a deck of cards face down on the table or floor.

2. Take turns with the other players to pick up two cards. If the cards have the same number or picture, you can keep them and take another turn. If they are not a pair, you put the cards back *exactly where you found them.* Then it is the next player's turn.

3. Whoever collects the most pairs at the end of the game is the winner.

Pay for a king!

This is a fun card game for two people to play.

1. Divide a deck of cards between the two players. Each player's cards are put face down in a pile in front of them.

2. Players take it in turns to place one card face up onto a central pile.

3. If one player turns over an Ace, King, Queen, or Jack, the other player has to pay for them like this:
Jack = one card
Queen = two cards
King = three cards
Ace = four cards

4. The player who is paying turns over this number of cards onto the central pile, one by one. If no royal cards or aces come up, the other player takes the whole central pile and puts it at the bottom of his own pile. But if another royal card or ace comes up during payment, he must now pay instead.

5. Sometimes the central pile of cards gets really big before either player wins it. The player who ends up with all the cards wins.

NOTE

This game can go on for a long time—or it can be over very quickly!

Birthday cards to make and give

Cut out cards

You need:
cardboard about
    8 inches x 6 inches
a pencil
scissors
crayons or colored
    pencils

1. Fold the cardboard firmly down the center. Use it with the fold at the top.

2. Draw a picture on the card, making sure that the drawing goes right up to the fold. Color your drawing. Cut around the drawing and your card will stand up.

NOTE

You can stick on glitter and bits of colored paper to make the card even brighter.

56

Lambs and clouds

This is a good card for someone with a springtime birthday.

You need:

cardboard about
    8 inches x 6 inches
crayons or colored
    pencils
absorbent cotton
glue

1. Fold the cardboard in half. Draw a picture of lambs in a field with clouds floating in the sky. Color your picture.

2. Stick puffs of cotton on the lambs' bodies and puffs of cotton on the shapes of the clouds.

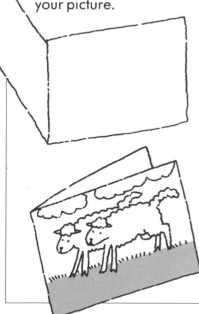

3. Write your birthday greeting inside the card.

NOTE

If you paint the absorbent cotton other colors, you can use it to make yellow ducklings and brown, fluffy rabbits.

Make a zigzag number book

A zigzag number book will stand on the shelf so that you can see all the numbers at once.

You need:
a long strip of
 thin cardboard
crayons or felt-tip
 pens

4. Stand your number book up on the shelf so that you can look at all the numbers.

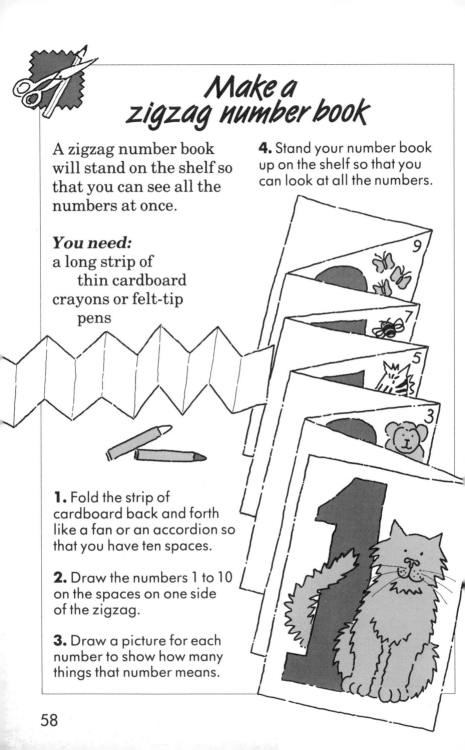

1. Fold the strip of cardboard back and forth like a fan or an accordion so that you have ten spaces.

2. Draw the numbers 1 to 10 on the spaces on one side of the zigzag.

3. Draw a picture for each number to show how many things that number means.

Make a pirate hat

Dress up as a pirate in this black pirate hat.

You need:

black construction paper
    17 inches x 7 inches
a pencil
scissors
glue, tape, or a stapler
white paint
a paint brush

1. Fold the black paper in half. Draw and cut out the two pirate hat shapes.

2. Stick the two hat pieces together firmly at the sides. Use glue, tape, or staples.

3. With the white paint, make a skull and crossbones on the front of the hat. This is the pirate sign.

NOTE

Make an eyepatch from a piece of black paper threaded on a thin elastic thread or a piece of string. You could also dangle a curtain ring from one ear to complete the pirate look.

MUSICAL GAMES

Turn on some music and play these games with your friends.

Statues

Everyone dances while the music plays. When the music stops, everyone stands as still as a statue. Anyone who moves is OUT.

Pass the package

Wrap a small prize in layers of paper. While the music plays, the players pass the package around in a circle. Each time the music stops, the person holding the package takes off one layer of paper.

Musical bumps

Everyone dances while the music plays. When the music stops, everyone drops down onto the floor. The last one down is OUT.

NOTE

Taped music is best for these games as it is easy to stop and start.

Musical islands

Place some pieces of cardboard around the floor of the room. You need one piece fewer than the number of players. While the music plays, everyone dances. As soon as the music stops, they must step onto one of the "islands." Only one person is allowed on an island. The person who is left without an island is OUT.

Take away an island each time the music starts up again.

INDEX

Things to make

In the kitchen

Action games

See how it works

Board and table games